SCHOLASTIC

AF668003

BOB BOOKS®

Developing Readers Workbook

Complex Words (K-1)

Ask for Bob Books® at your local bookstore, or visit www.bobbooks.com.

No part of this publication may be reproduced, stored in a retrieval system, or transmitted in any form or by any means, electronic, mechanical, photocopying, recording, or otherwise, without written permission of the publisher. For information regarding permission, write to Scholastic Inc., Attention: Permissions Department, 557 Broadway, New York, NY 10012.

ISBN 978-93-5471-668-3

Copyright © 2022 by Bob Books Publications, LLC. All rights reserved. Published by Scholastic Inc., *Publishers since 1920.* By arrangement with Bob Books® Publications, LLC. SCHOLASTIC and associated logos are trademarks and/or registered trademarks of Scholastic Inc. Bob Books and associated logos are trademarks and/or registered trademarks of Bob Books Publications, LLC.

Printed in India

This reprint edition, August 2025

Bob Books: Complex Words
Workbook

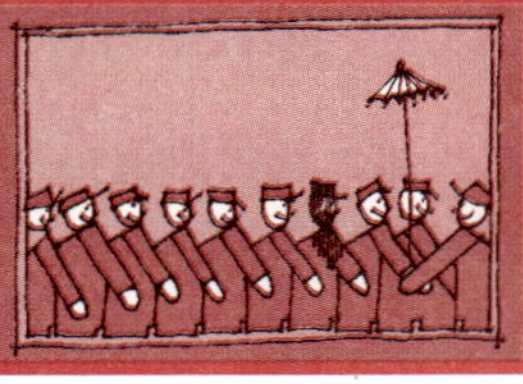

Ten Men

Read the story and colour each picture. Then circle the words in each sentence that have a short "e" sound, as in "hen."

Ten Men

Hand in hand they went.

They went in wind.

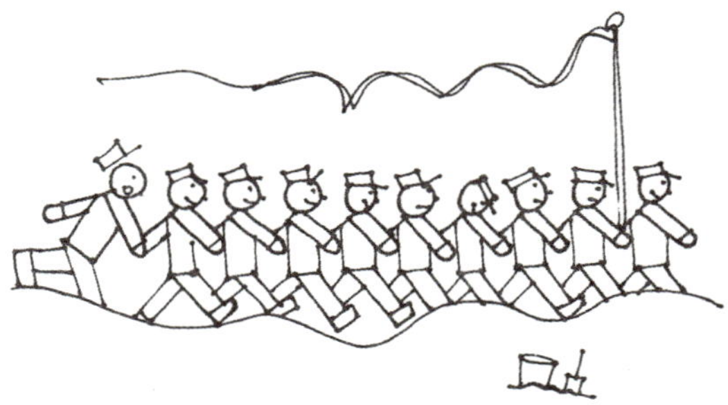

They went in sand.

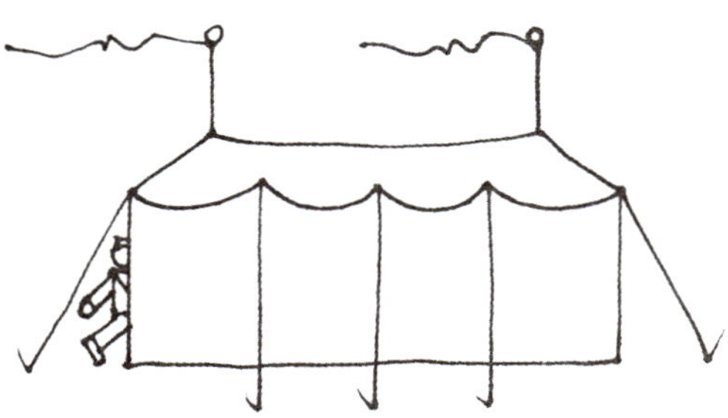

Into a tent
the ten men went.

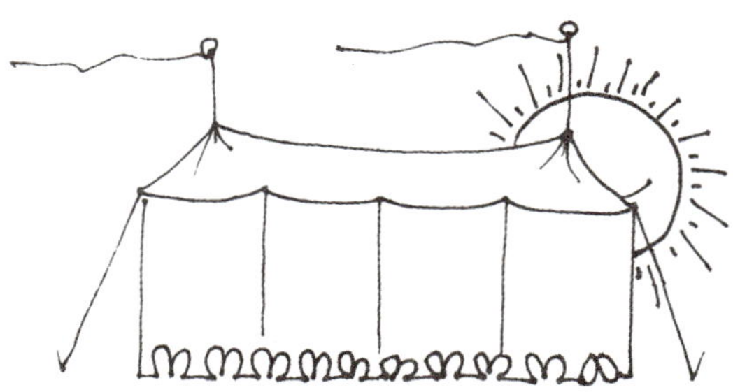

The sun has set on
the ten and the tent.

Say and write the words.

tent — tent

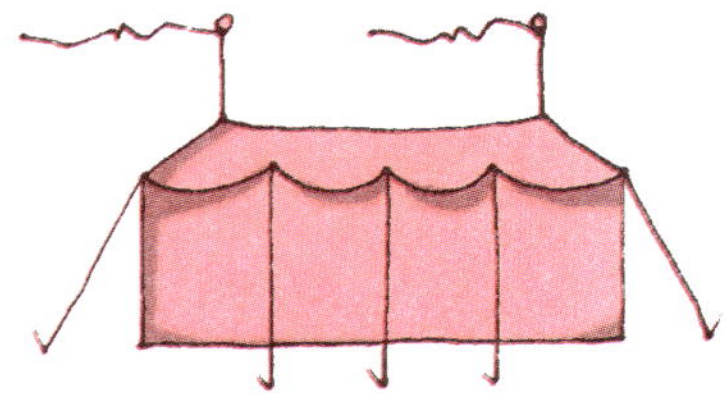

flag

end

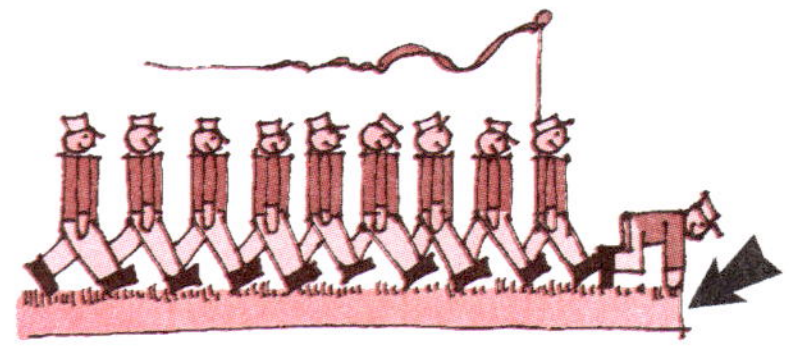

drum

hand

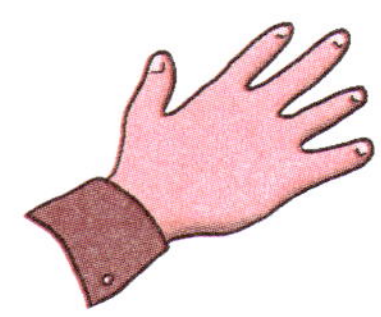

wind

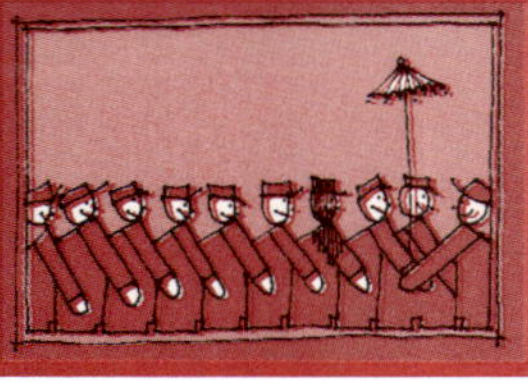

Ten Men

Read each clue and complete the crossword.

Clues

1
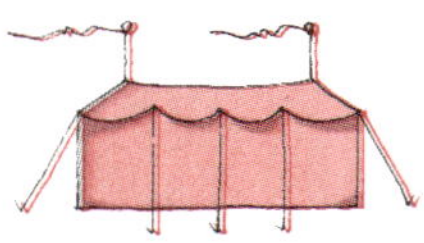

2
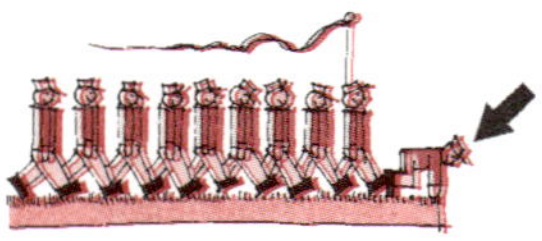

3

4
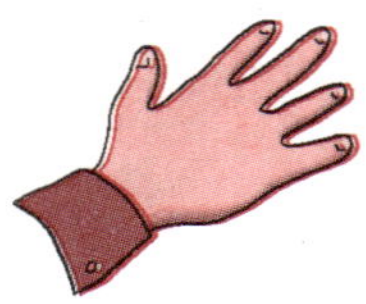

5

6

Word Bank

bend tent Fred flag clock
drum hand wind end jump

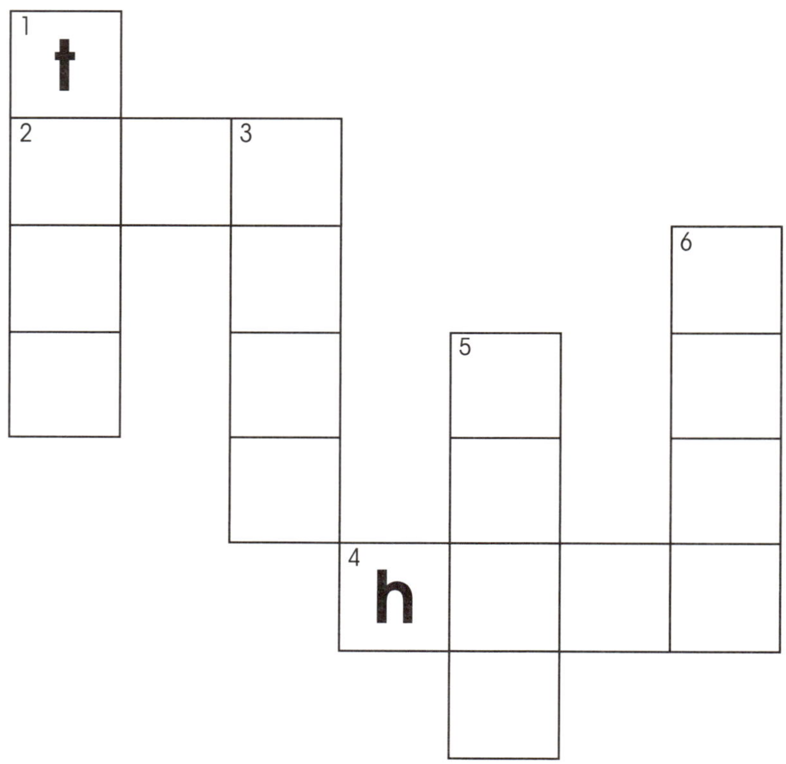

Fill in the missing letters to complete the sentences.

They went in wi___ ___.

They went in sa___ ___.

Jim had a ___ ___um.

Hand in ha___ ___
they went.

Tim had a ___ ___ag.

Ten men went to the
e___ ___ of the land.

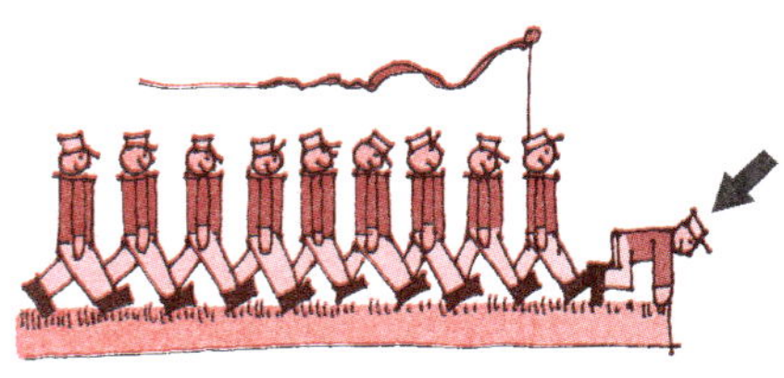

Ten Men

Circle the words with the **short "e"** sound.
Connect the circles to make a path.

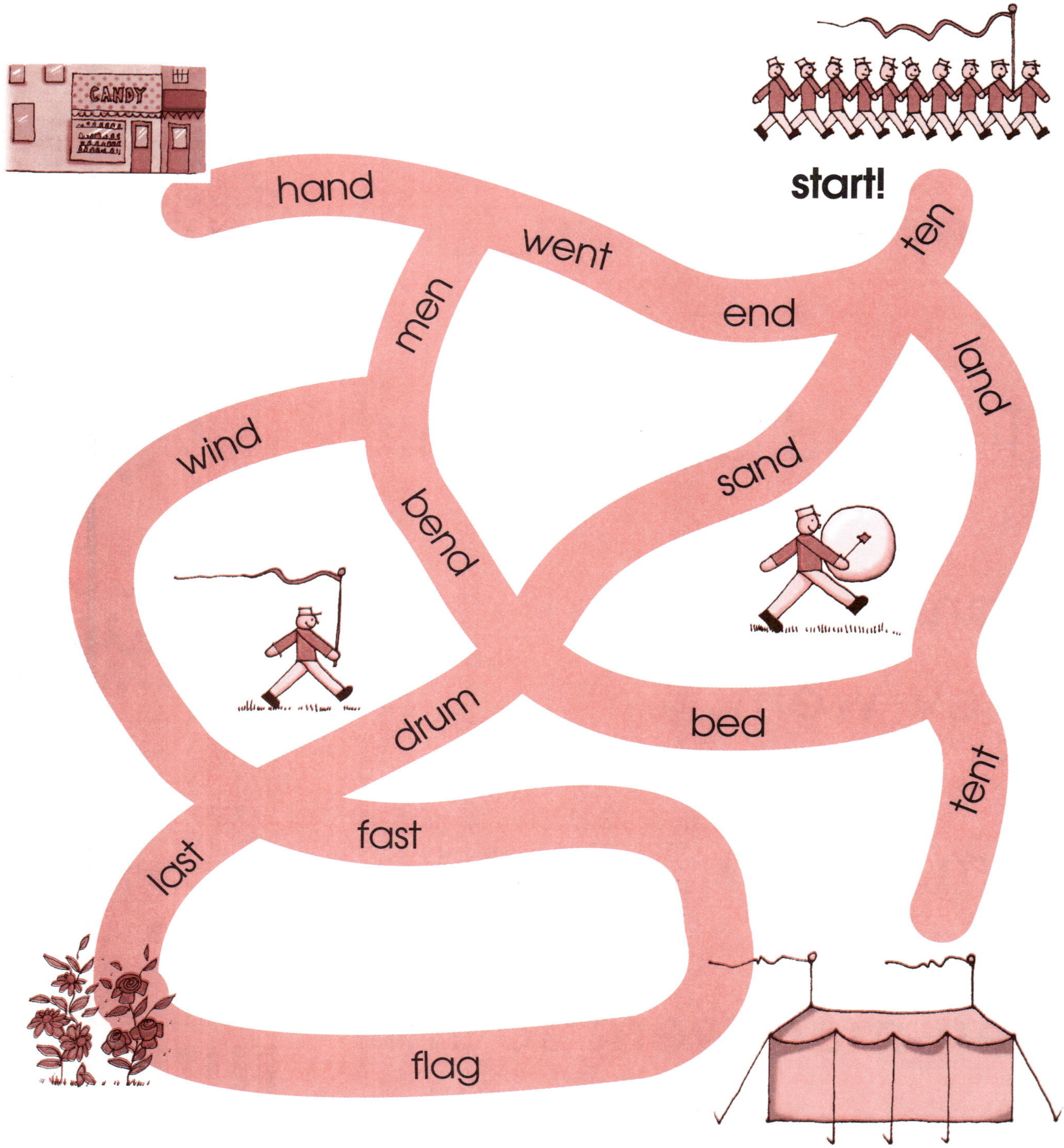

Draw a line to the correct word, then write it.

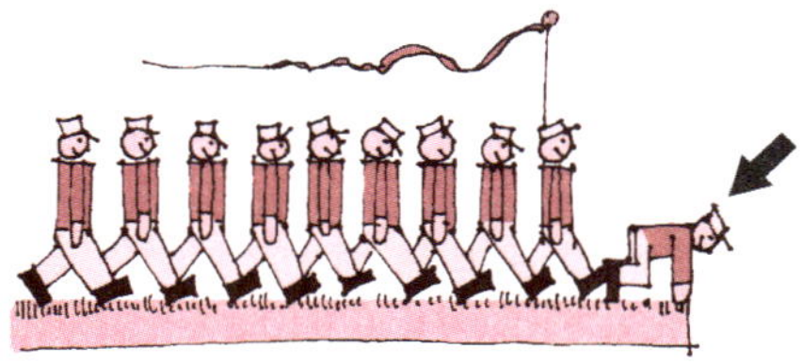

Ten men went to the ________ of the land.

end

bend

Tim went ________ .

last

fast

Hand in hand they ________ .

went

tent

Tim had a ________ .

flag

frog

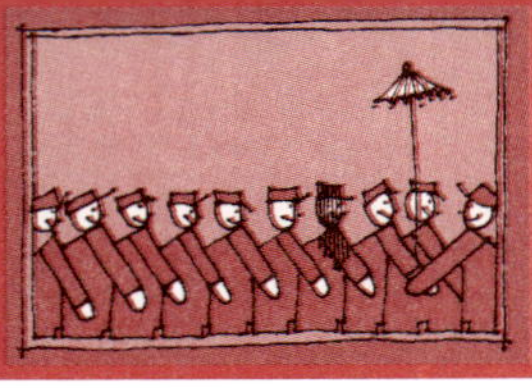

Ten Men

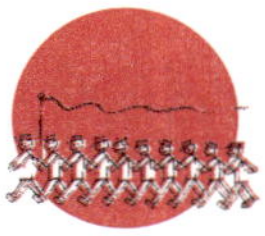

Make complete sentences using the words from box A and box B.

Box A	Box B
Tim	went in sand.
They	had a drum.
Jim	went fast.

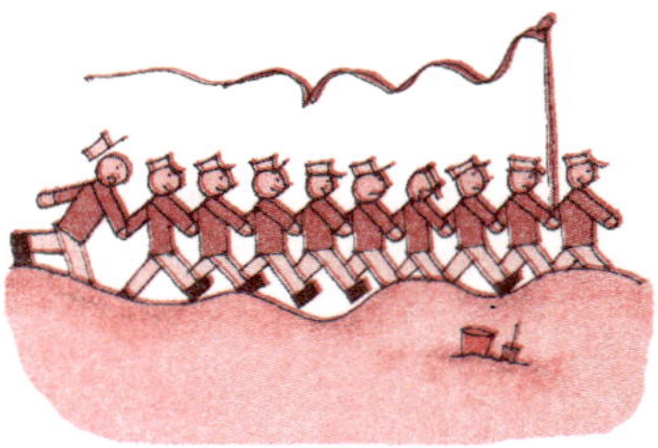

Draw a line from each picture to the correct consonant blend. Fill in the blank.

a nt

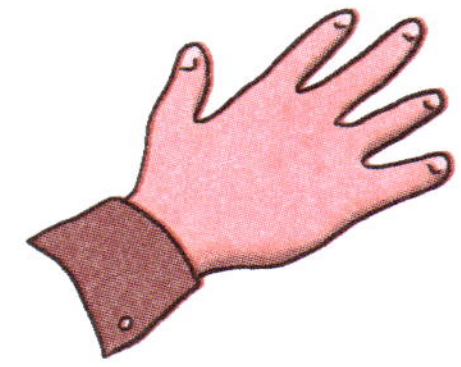

ha

nt

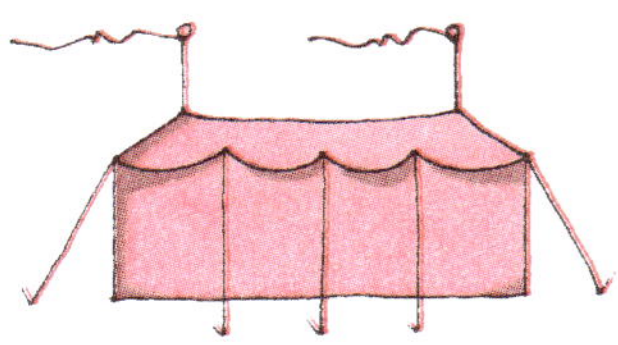

te

po

nd

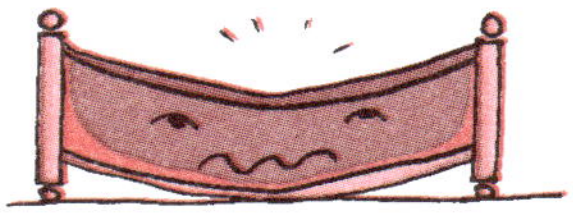

be

ce

Bump!

Read the story and colour each picture. Then circle the words in each sentence that have a short "u" sound, as in "bug."

Bump!

Sunny jumped.

Skipper and Thumper bumped!

Sunny and Thumper jumped up.

Skipper slipped.

Jimmy and Skipper skipped.

Say and write the words.

bump bump

jump

slip

over

Thumper

Jimmy

Bump!

Read each clue and complete the crossword.

Clues

1 

2 

3 

4 

5 

6 

Word Bank

six bump up slip Thumper
over fish jump fun Jimmy

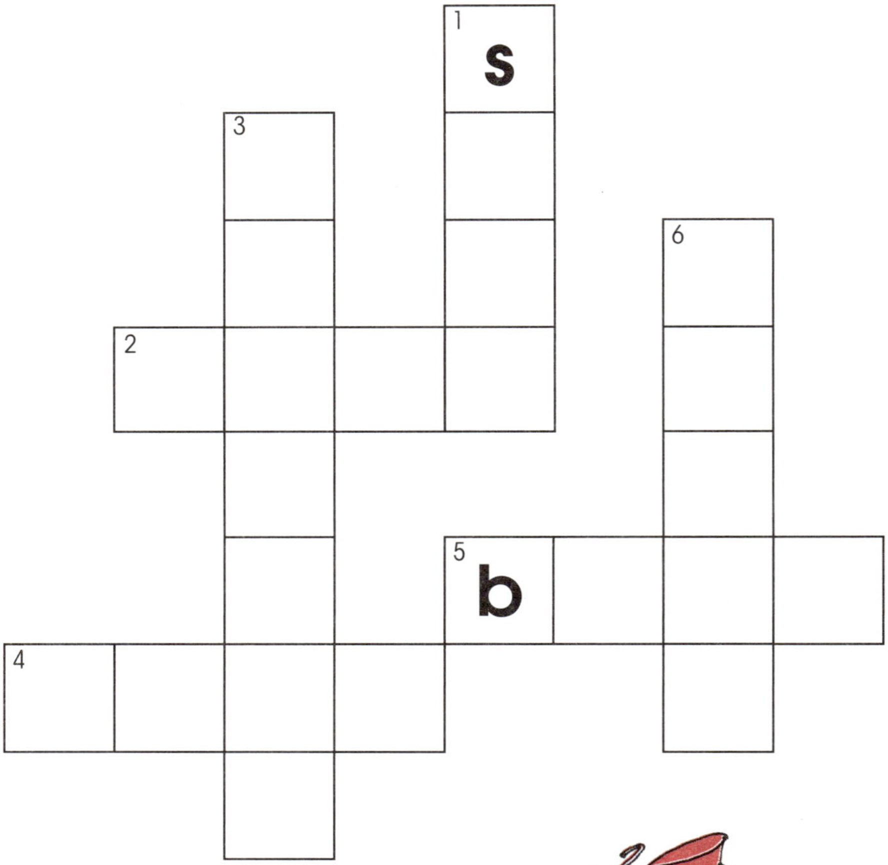

Fill in the missing letters to complete the sentence.

Sunny ju___ ___ed.

Thumper skipp___ ___.

Skipper ___ ___ipped.

Skipper and Thumper
bu___ ___ed!

___ ___umper jumped.

Bump!

Circle the words with the **short "u"** sound.
Connect the circles to make a path.

Draw a line to the correct word, then write it.

Jimmy ______________ .

jumped

bumped

Skipper jumped

and ______________ .

dripped

skipped

____________ and Thumper

jumped up.

Jimmy

Sunny

Skipper ______________ .

slipped

stopped

Bump!

Make complete sentences using the words from box A and box B.

Box A	Box B
Skipper	bumped!
Skipper and Thumper	slipped.
Jimmy and Skipper	jumped over.

Draw a line from each picture to the correct consonant blend. Fill in the blank.

bu ☐

re ☐

fa ☐

st

ve ☐

mp

la ☐

ju ☐

Cat and Mouse

Read the story and colour each picture. Then circle the words in each sentence that have a short "a" sound, as in "apple."

Cat and Mouse

Tilly sat by the mouse house.

The mouse ran out of his house.

The cat went slam, slap, snap!

"Help! Help! Stop that cat!"

The mouse is happy to be back in his house.

Say and write the words.

mouse mouse

house

kitty

sit

flip

skip

Cat and Mouse

Read each clue and complete the crossword.

Clues

1. 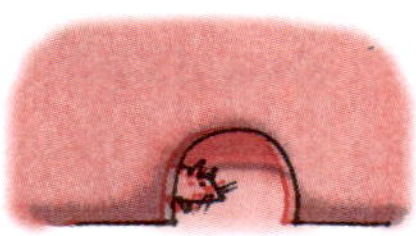
2. 
3. 
4. 
5. 
6. 

Word Bank

mouse pond house kitty flip
fox skip duck sit Jimmy

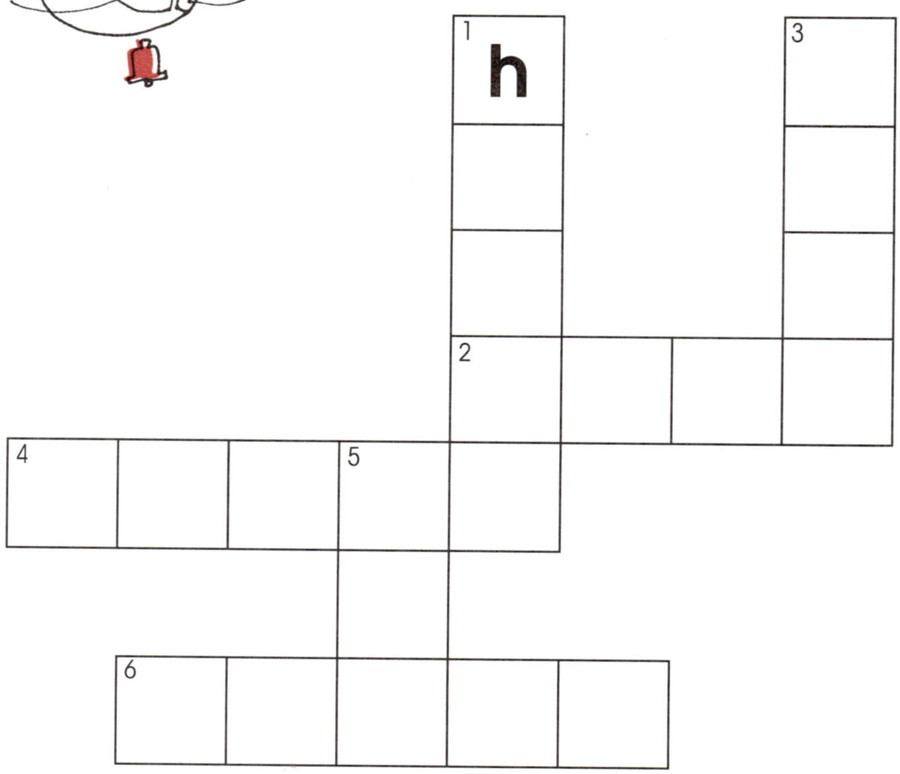

Fill in the missing letters to complete the sentence.

The cat is ___ ___ppy.

The cat ___ ___ nt slam slap, snap!

The mouse is happy to be ba___ ___ in his house.

"Help! He___ ___!
___ ___op that cat!"

Tilly went ___ ___ip flop.

Cat and Mouse

Circle the words with the **short "a"** sound.
Connect the circles to make a path.

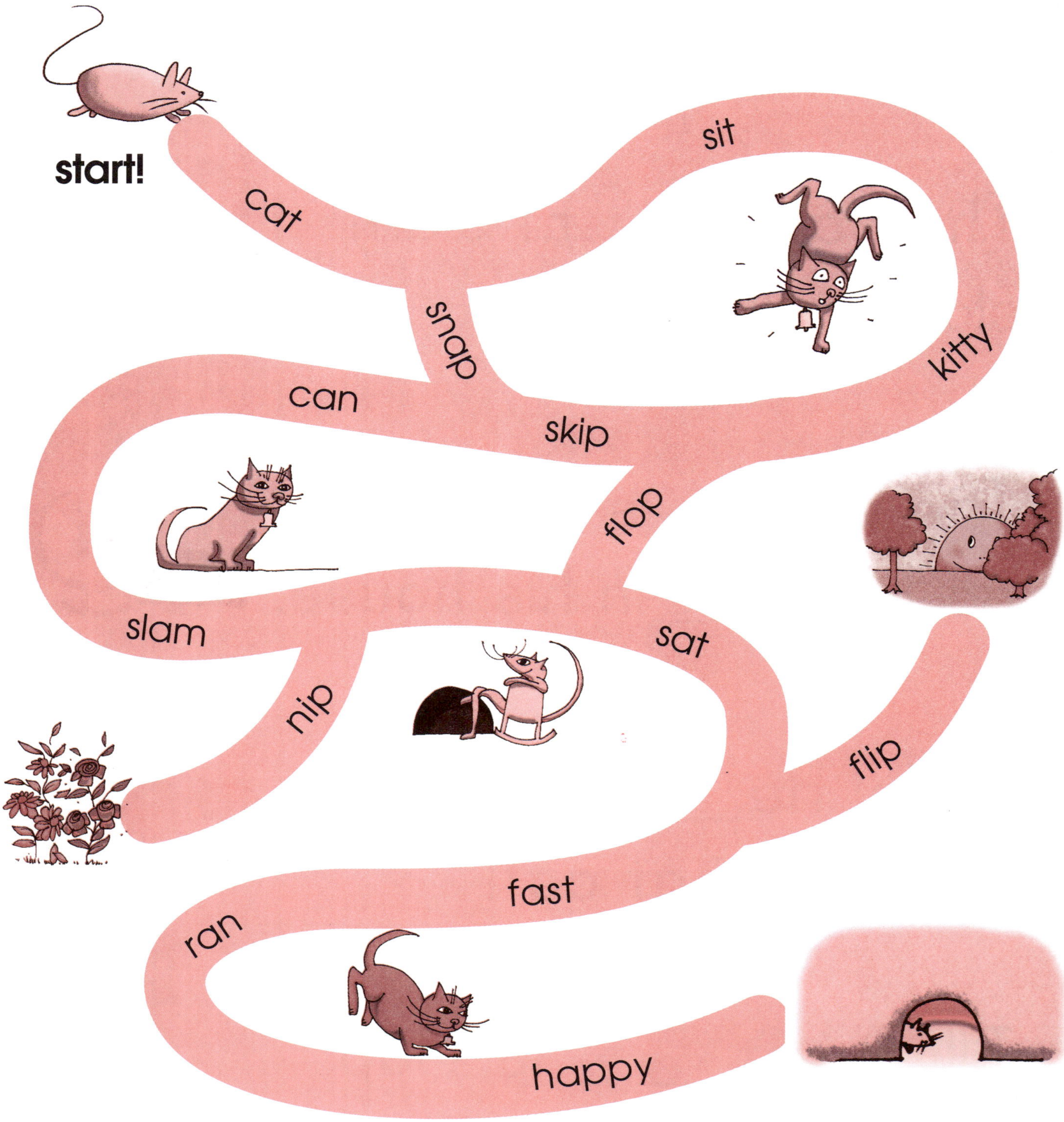

Draw a line to the correct word, then write it.

Tilly is a __________ cat.

happy

kitty

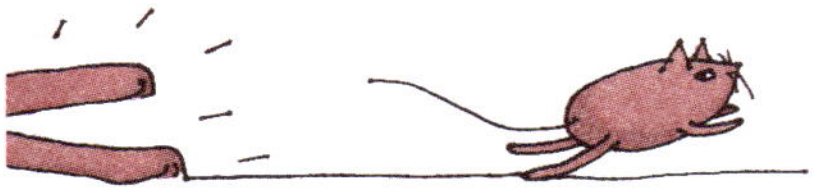

The __________ ran faster.

house

mouse

"Help! Help! __________ that cat!"

Stop

Step

Tilly went __________ flop.

flag

flip

Cat and Mouse

Make complete sentences using the words from box A and box B.

Box A	Box B
The cat	is in his house.
A mouse	can skip.
Tilly	went flip-flop.

Draw a line from each picture to the correct consonant blend. Fill in the blank.

☐ ip

☐ ag

☐ y

fl

sk

☐ ip

☐ unk

☐ y

The Swimmers

Read the story and colour each picture. Then circle the words in each sentence that have a short "o" sound, as in "mop."

The Swimmers

It was summer.
Pop, Stan, and Jim went to the pond.

Jim slipped into the pond. Stan jumped into the pond.

"Step on the log, Jim," called Stan. Jim slipped.

"Stop! Stop!" called Pop.
The log spun.

The three swimmers went to a sunny spot.

Say and write the words.

swam swam

help

spun

slid

wet

sunny

The Swimmers

Read each clue and complete the crossword.

Clues

1

2
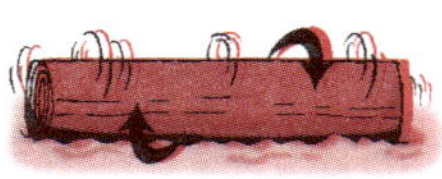

3

4

5
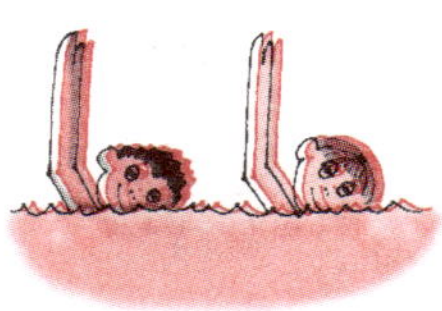

6

Word Bank

sunny help push spun swam
shop slid flew wet pal

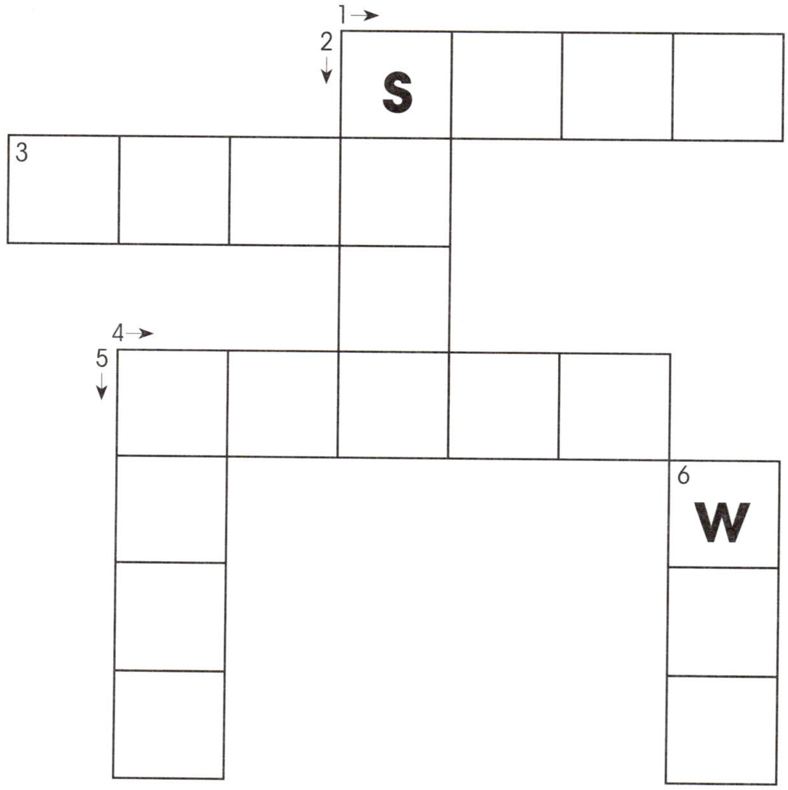

Fill in the missing letters to complete the sentence.

Jim and Stan wanted to ___ ___im.

Jim ___ ___ipped into the pond.

Pop wanted to he___ ___ Jim and Stan.

Stan ___ ___id.

"___ ___ep on the log, Jim," called Stan.

The Swimmers

Circle the words with the **short "o"** sound.
Connect the circles to make a path.

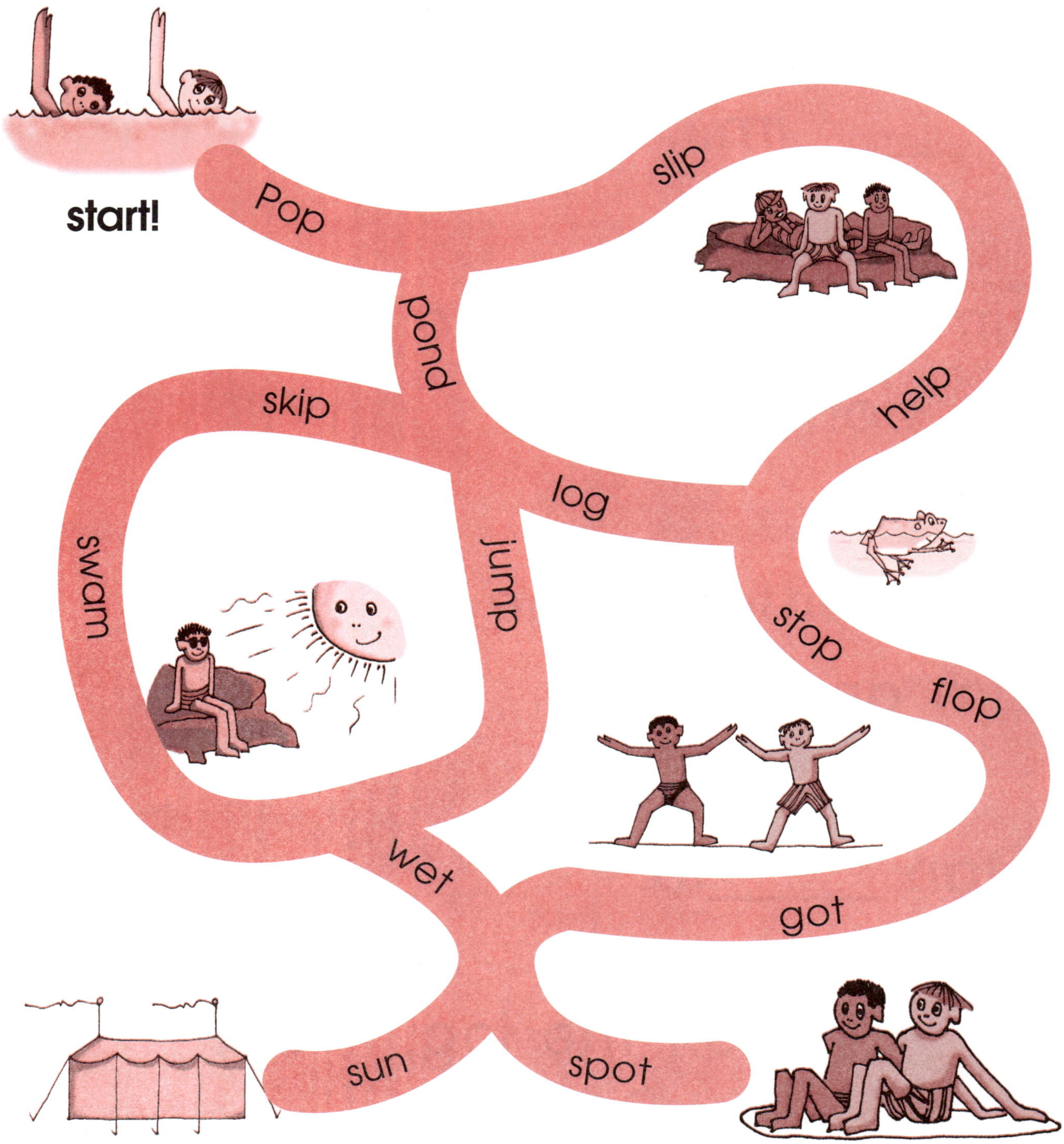

Draw a line to the correct word, then write it.

Pop, Stan, and Jim went to the __________ .

sand

pond

Jim and Stan __________ to a log.

swam

slid

The log __________ .

spot

spun

The three swimmers went to a __________ spot.

sunny

funny

The Swimmers

Make complete sentences using the words from box A and box B.

Box A	Box B
Pop	spun.
Jim and Stan	swam to a log.
The log	got wet.

Draw a line from each picture to the correct consonant blend. Fill in the blank.

[ ] id

[ ] un

[ ] ot

sp

sl

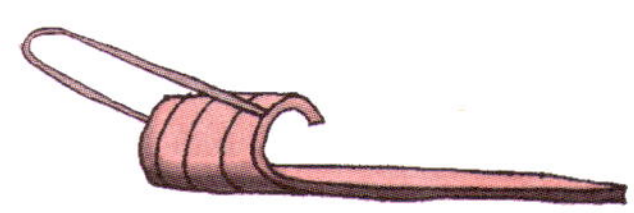

[ ] ed

[ ] ip

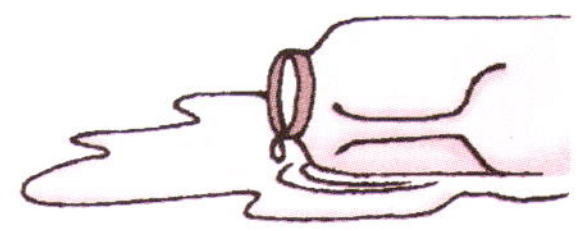

[ ] ill

Samantha

Read the story and colour each picture. Then circle the words in each sentence that have a short "i" sound, as in "sit."

Samantha

Mama cooked eggs.

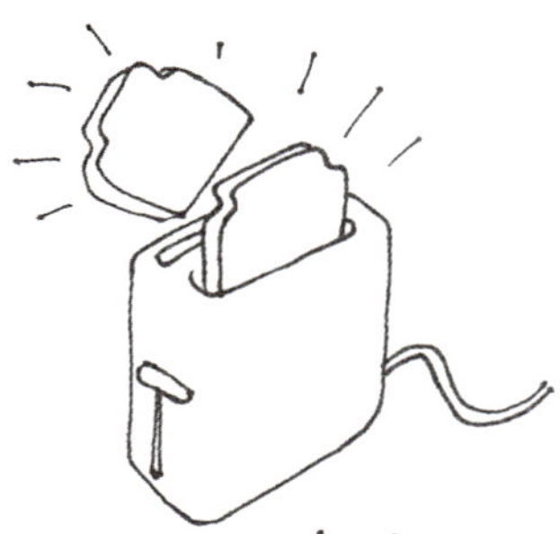

Toast popped from the toaster.

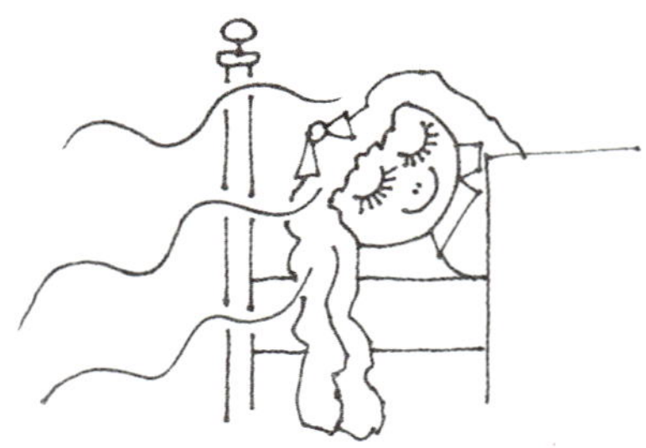

The smells whiffed into Samantha's room.

Her nose sniffed and sniffed. She licked her lips.

"Good morning," said the bright sunlight.

Match each word to the correct picture.

smell •

sniff •

morning •

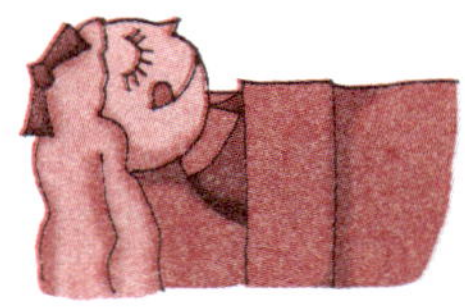

lick •

bark •

tweet •

Samantha

Read each clue and complete the crossword.

Clues

1

2

3

4

5

6

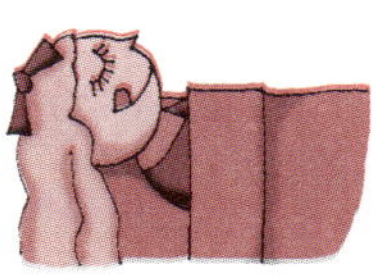

Word Bank

morning	bed	smell	pup	sniff
toast	tweet	lip	bark	lick

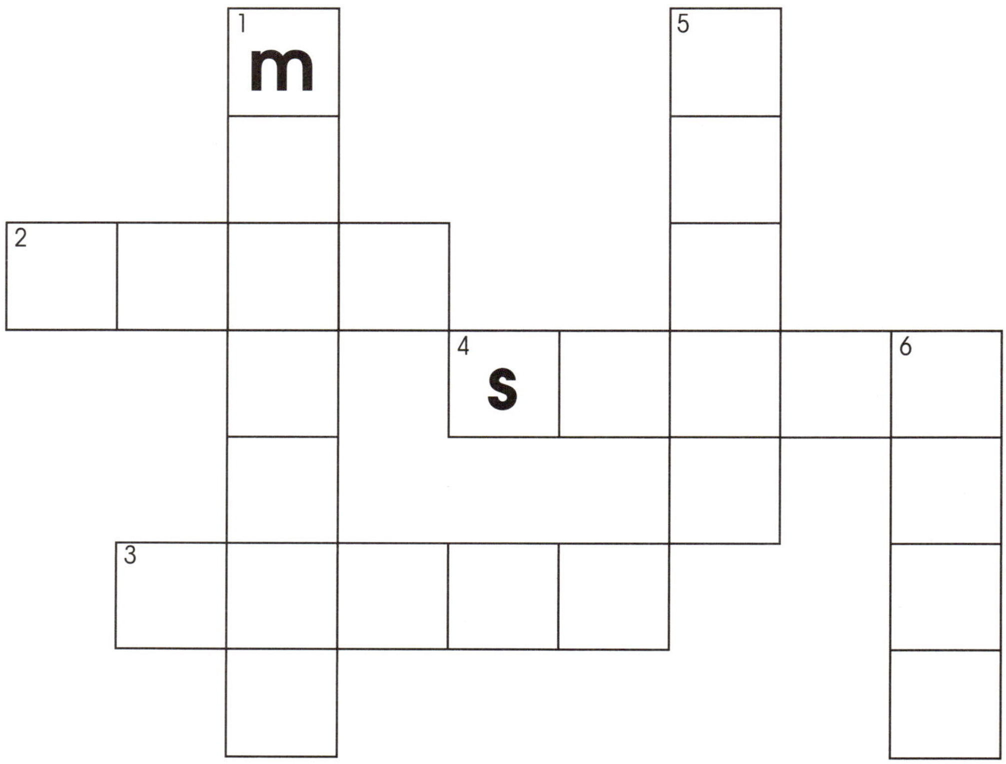

Fill in the missing letters to complete the sentence.

The smells ___ ___iffed into Samantha's room.

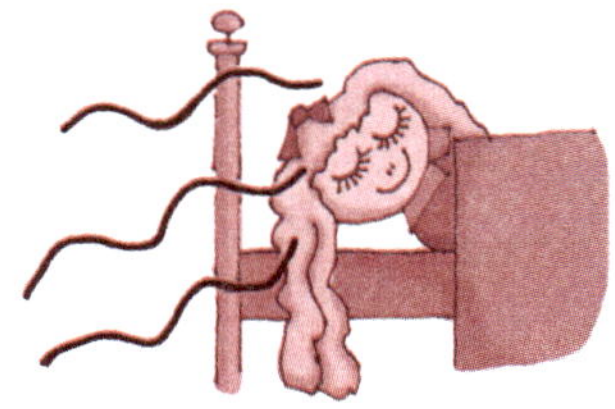

She li___ ___ed her lips.

"Good mo___ ___ing, Mama and Papa," she said.

"Woof! Woof!" ba___ ___ed Roofus.

"Good morn___ ___ ___," said the bright sunlight.

Samantha

Circle the words ending with **"ed."**
Connect the circles to make a path.

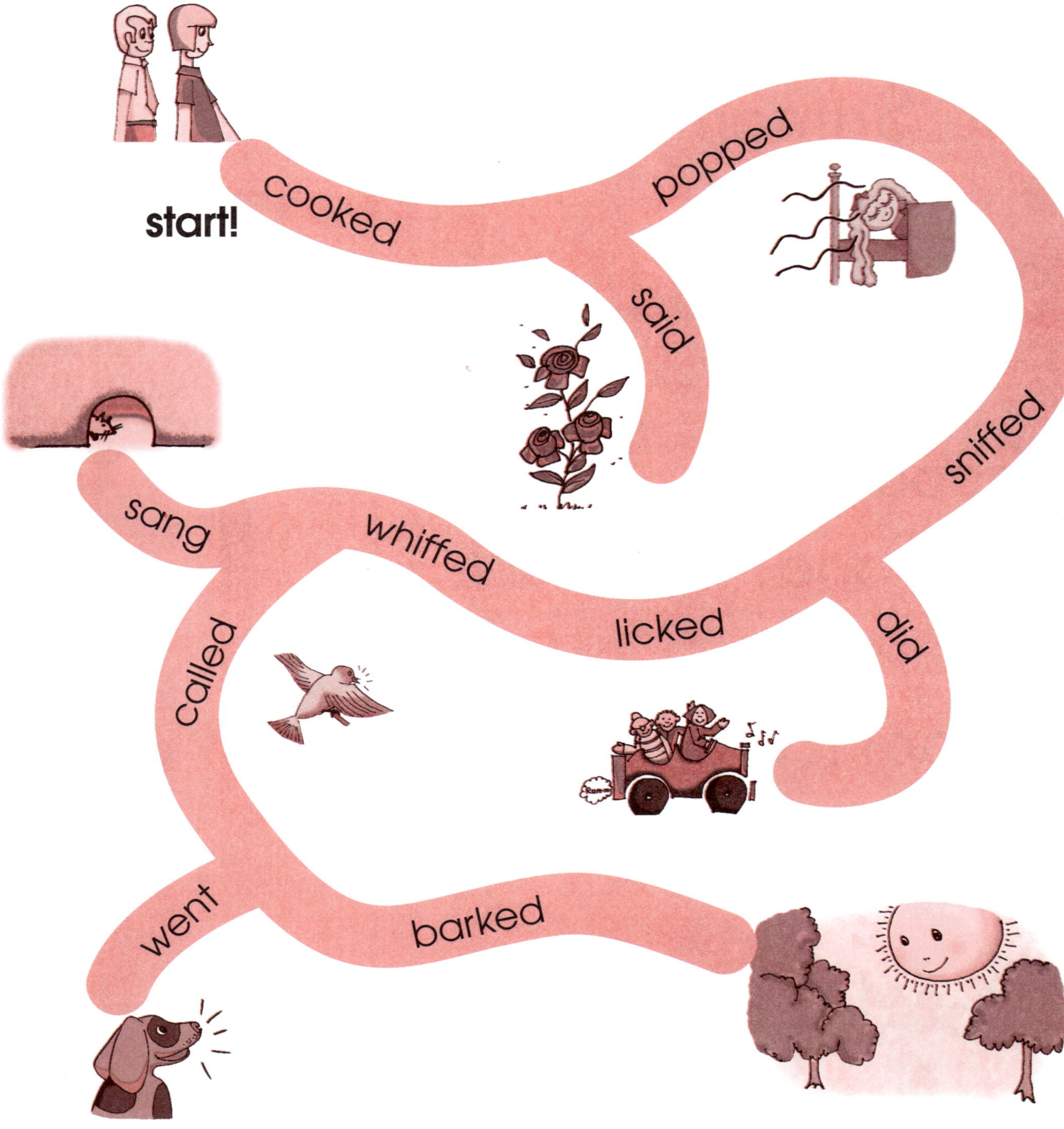

Draw a line to the correct word, then write it.

" _____________ tight, Samantha," said Mama.

Sleep

Slap

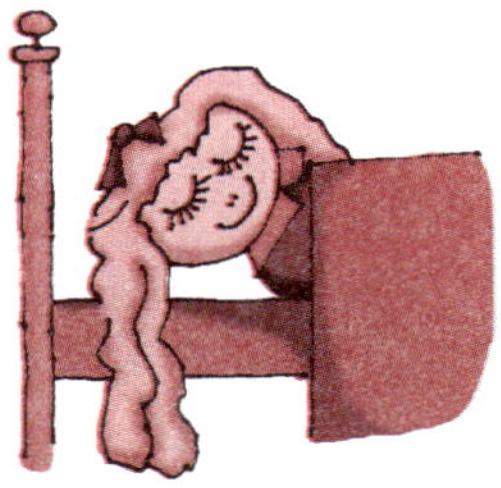

Samantha was _________ in bed.

still

lost

"Woof! Woof!" ____________ Roofus.

barked

started

"Good _____________ ," said the bright sunlight.

horn

morning

Samantha

Put the words in the correct order to make the sentences.

her lips licked She

___ l_____

h__ ____.

sun The set

___ s__ ___.

eggs Mama cooked

____ ______

e___.

Circle and write the correct consonant blend for each picture.

sm ell

st sm sk sl

ba ☐

rl lt rk lk

☐ iff

sp st sw sn

☐ eet

tw sw tr sr

Willy's Wish

Read the story and colour each picture. Then circle the words in each sentence that have a short "i" sound, as in "hit."

Willy's Wish

Willy threw three pennies into the wishing well.

Willy sat and sat. He put his chin on his hand. "I have a car. I have a cat."

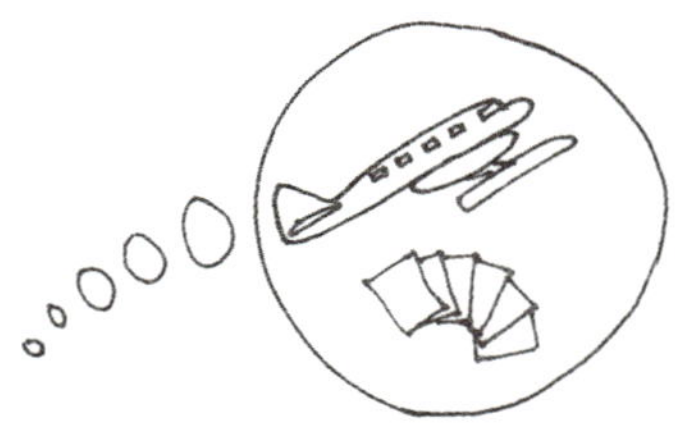

"I have a card game. I have a jet plane. What can I wish?"

He sniffed and sniffed.

Willy said, "I wish, I wish," as he licked his lips, "for a big, big dish of FISH AND CHIPS!"

Match each word to the correct picture.

wish

dish

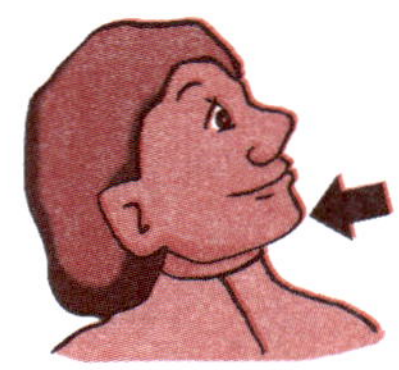

silk

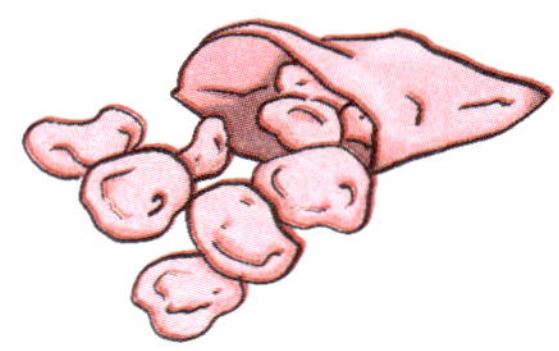

chin

chip

card

Willy's Wish

Read each clue and complete the crossword.

Clues

1

2
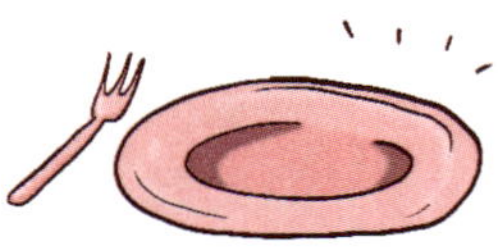

3

4

5
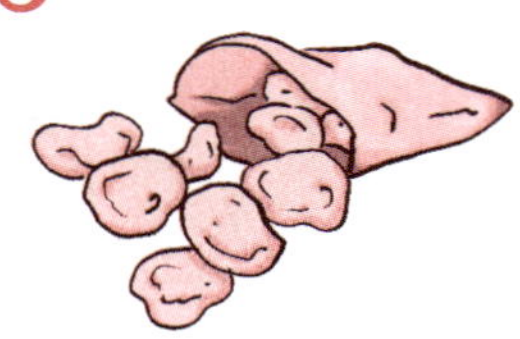

6
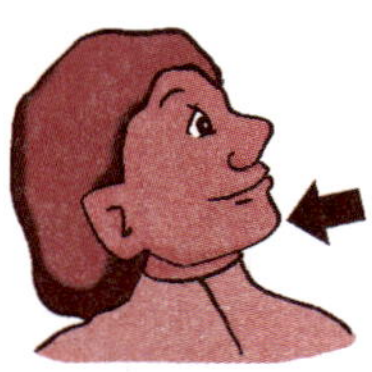

Word Bank

chin silk well dish think
wish card cap hand chip

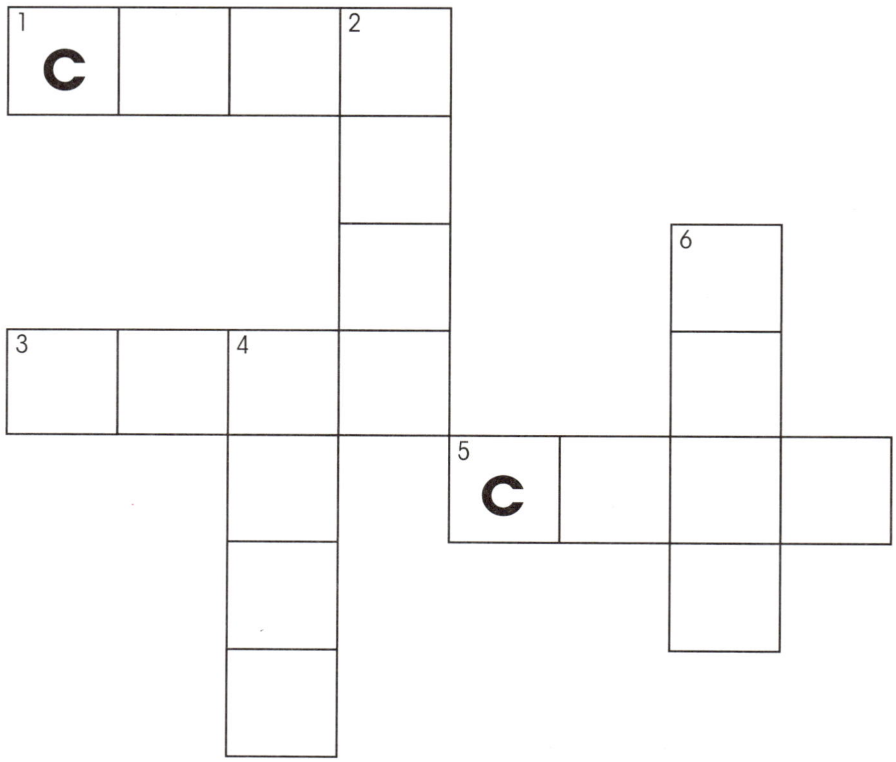

Fill in the missing letters to complete the sentence.

What do you wi__ __?

He put his __ __ in on his hand.

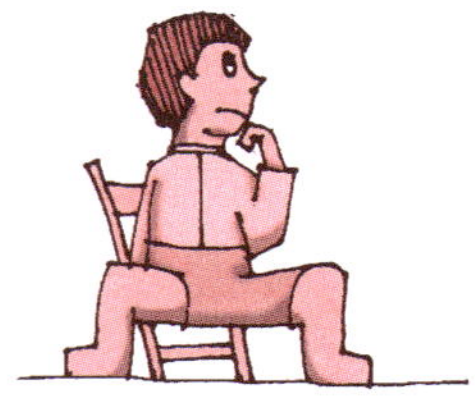

I have a ca__ __ game.

Fish and __ __ips.

His mama wished for a red si__ __ dress.

He li__ __ed his lips.

Willy's Wish

Circle the words with the **short "i"** sound.
Connect the circles to make a path.

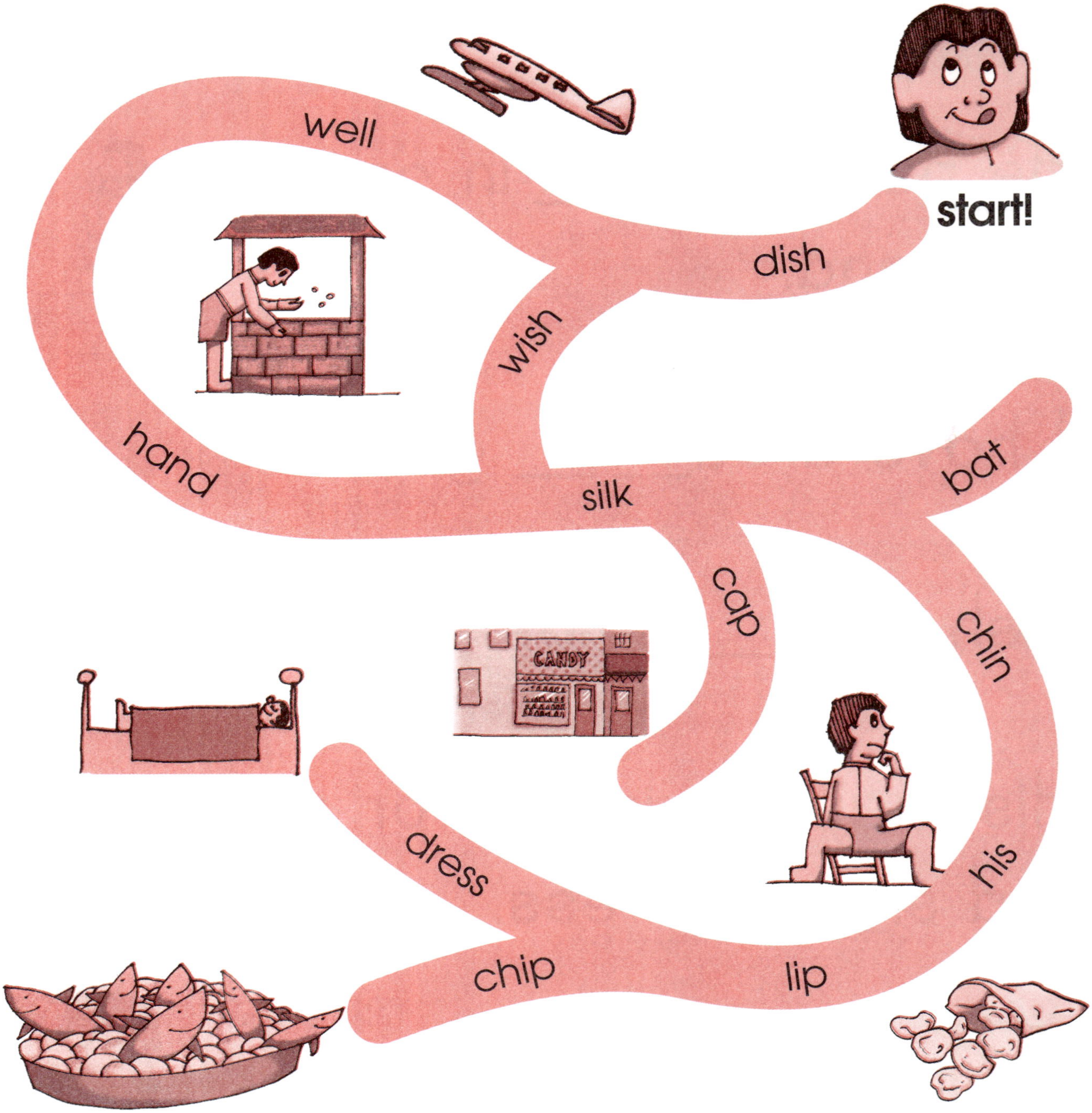

Draw a line to the correct word, then write it.

"What do you ________ ?"
his mama said.

wish

fish

"I cannot ________ ,"
is all he said.

threw

think

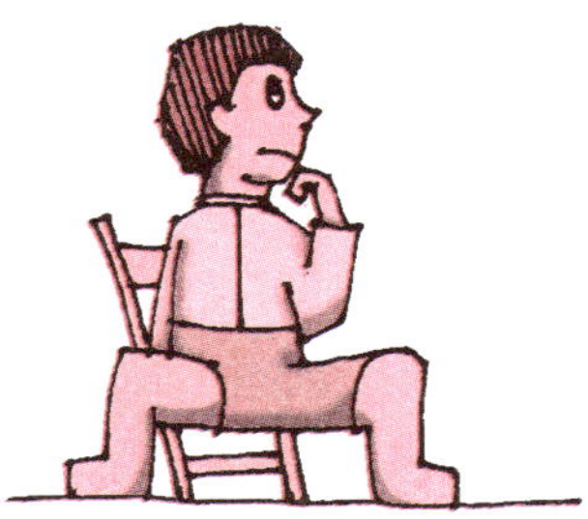

He put his ________
on his hand.

chip

chin

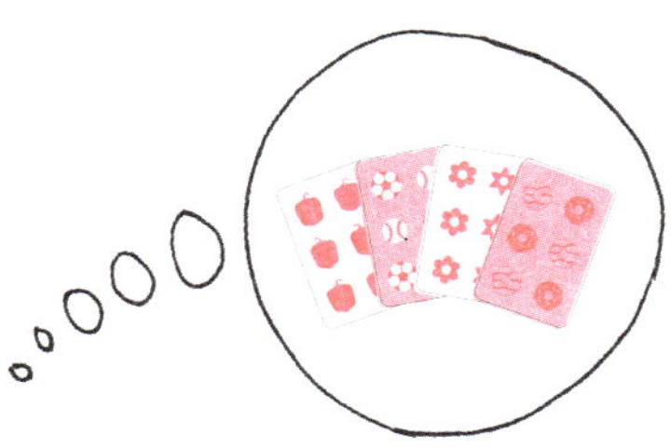

I have a ________ game.

card

car

Willy's Wish

Put the words in the correct order to make the sentences.

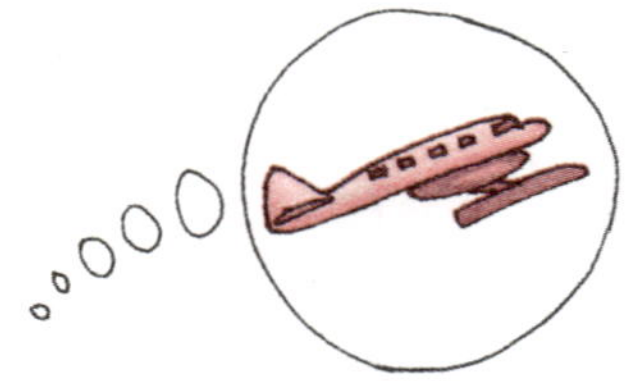

a I plane have jet

_ h _ _ _ _ _ _ _ _

p _ _ _ _.

wish do What you

_ _ _ _ _ _ _ _ _

w _ _ _?

lips licked He his

_ _ _ _ _ _ _ _

h _ _ _ _ _ _.

Circle and write the correct consonant blend for each picture.

[ ] in

sh   ch   ck   th

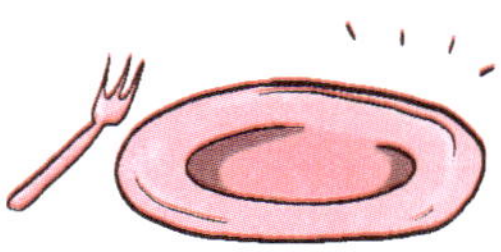

di [ ]

wh   ph   ch   sh

ca [ ]

rd   lk   rl   nd

wi [ ]

ng   sh   ll   ck

Jumper and the Clown

Read the story and colour each picture. Then circle the words in each sentence that have a short "a" sound, as in "pat."

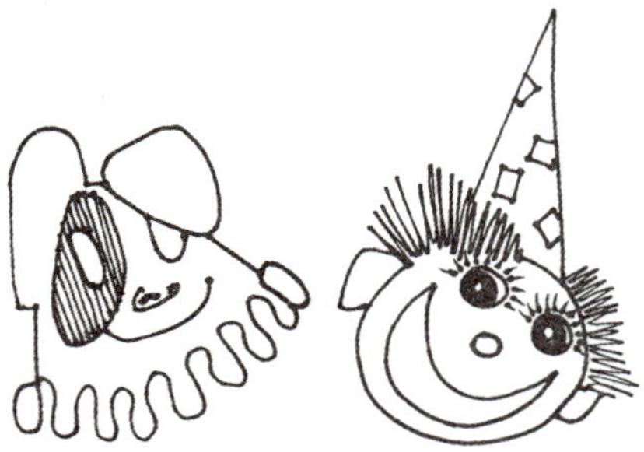

Jumper and the Clown

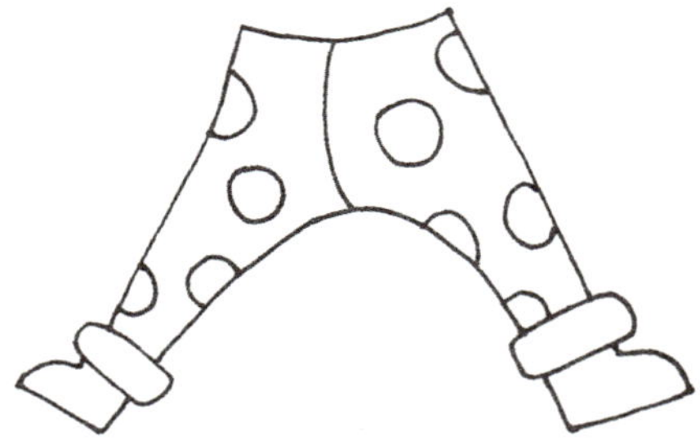

The clown had red pants with pink dots.

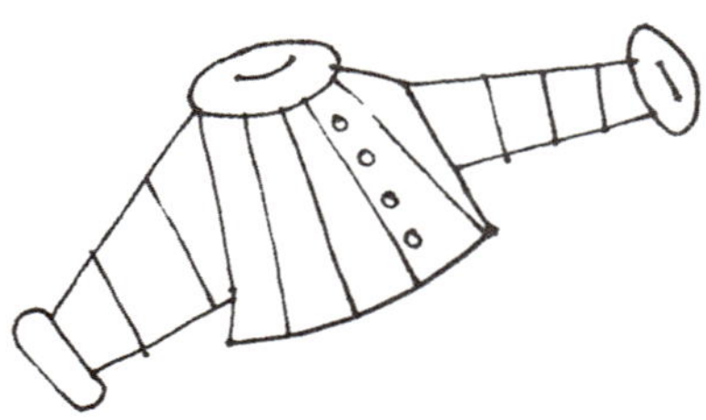

Her top was green and yellow.

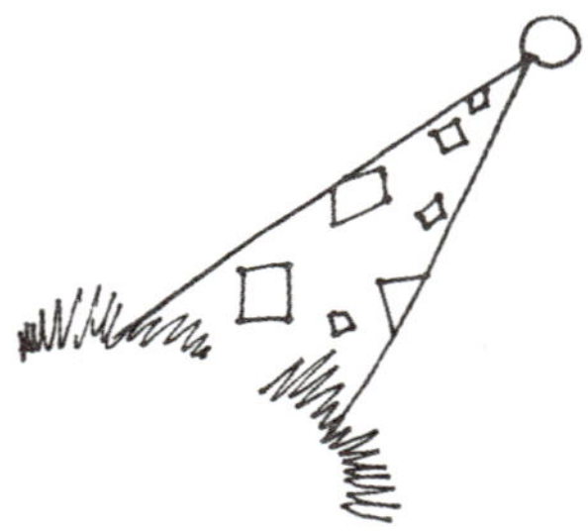

Her hat had spots of blue and orange.

She had a round red nose and a big grin. Her hair was purple.

With the clown was a little brown and black pup.

Match each word to the correct picture.

clown	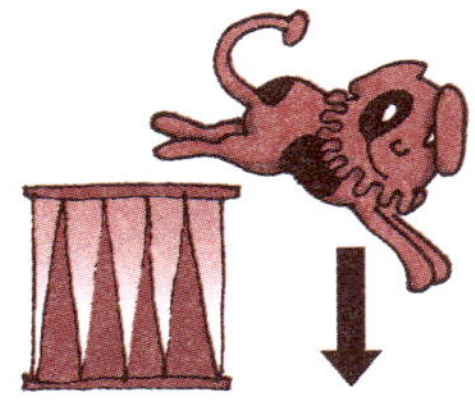
town	
brown	
grin	
down	
crown	

Jumper and the Clown

Read each clue and complete the crossword.

Clues

1

2

3

4

5

6

Word Bank

grin play crown pink town
down clown spot brown clap

Fill in the missing letters to complete the sentence.

A ___ ___own came to town!

Her top was ___ ___een and yellow.

With the clown was a little ___ ___own and ___ ___ack pup.

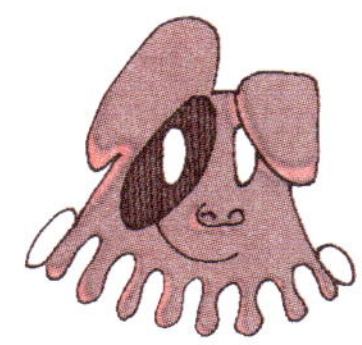

The clown grinned a big ___ ___in.

The clown had red pants with pi___ ___ dots.

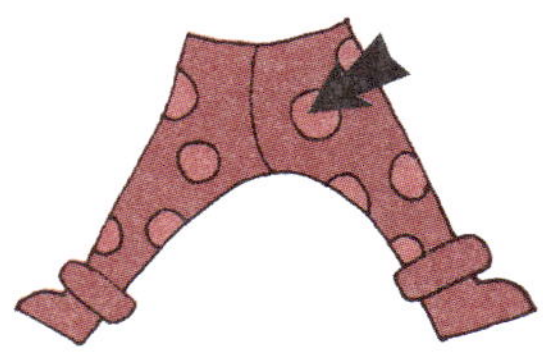

Jumper and the Clown

Circle the words with the **"ow"** sound.
Connect the circles to make a path.

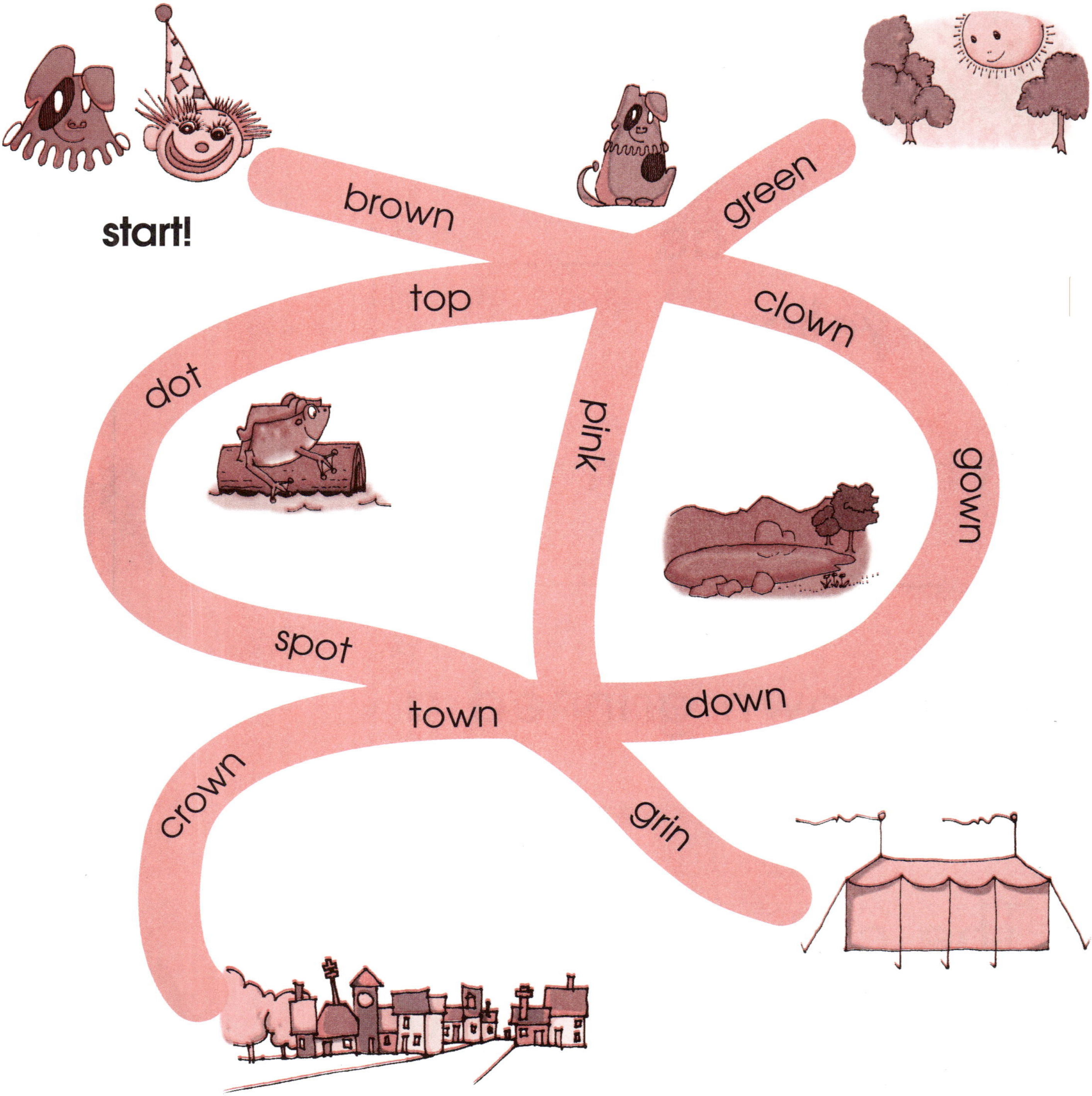

Draw a line to the correct word, then write it.

A clown came to ________ !

frown

town

She had a round red nose

and a big ________ .

spin

grin

With the clown was a little

________ and black pup.

brown

crown

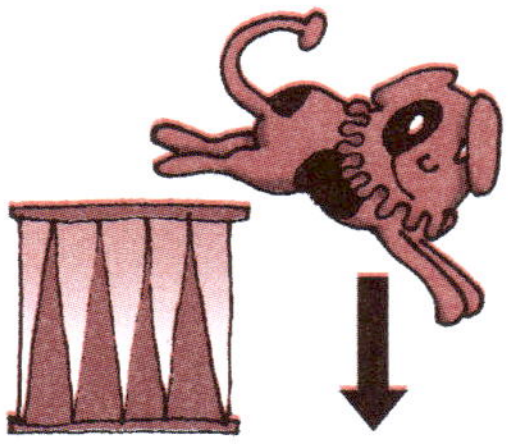

He jumped up.

He jumped ________ .

down

gown

Jumper and the Clown

Put the words in the correct order to make the sentences.

hair purple Her was

_ _ _   h _ _ _   _ _ _

p _ _ _ _ _.

was Jumper pup The called

_ _ _   _ _ _   w _ _

_ _ _ _ _ _   _ _ _ _ _ _.

clown to town A came

_   _ _ _ _ _   c _ _ _

_ _   _ _ _ _!

Circle and write the correct consonant blend for each picture.

☐ own

bl fl sl cl

Ju ☐ er

lp mp nk ft

☐ ane

pl dl fl gl

si ☐

lt lp lk nk

Max and the Tom Cats

Read the story and colour each picture. Then circle the words in each sentence that have a short "i" sound, as in "mit."

Max and the Tom Cats

Six tom cats sit on the tiptop of a big wall.

The sun will set soon.

Max, who is six, sits up in a tree.

"Hey, cats," calls Max, "what do you see?"

Max was glad he was in the tree to see the moonlight and to hear the song.

Match each word to the correct picture.

tree • 

moon • 

look • 

light • 

night • 

bright • 

Max and the Tom Cats

Read each clue and complete the crossword.

Clues

1 

2 

3 

4 

5 

6 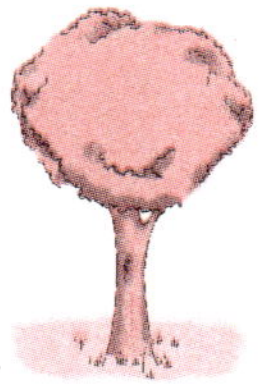

Word Bank

light	glad	bright	last	night
look	moon	song	tree	white

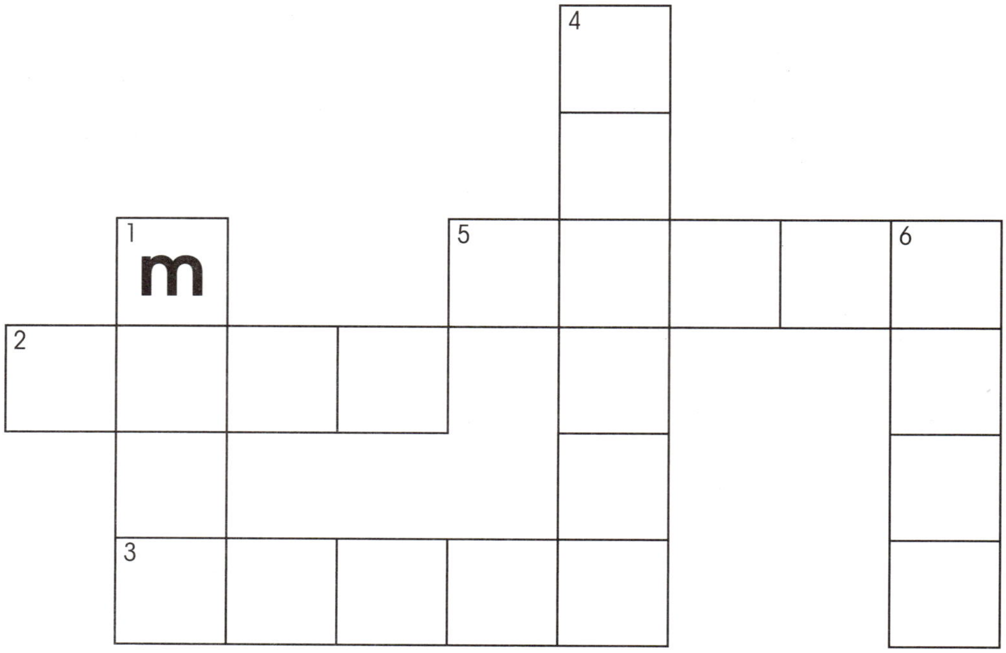

Fill in the missing letters to complete the sentence.

Max, who is six, sits up in a tr___ ___.

After a t___me the sun did set.

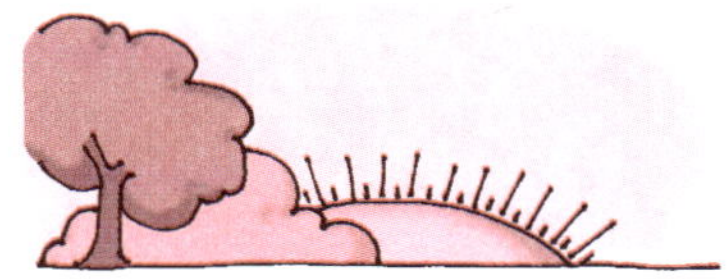

Max sat looking at the big wh___te moon.

The man in the m___ ___n saw six cats and Max.

Goodni___ ___ ___, Max.
Goodni___ ___ ___, Cats.

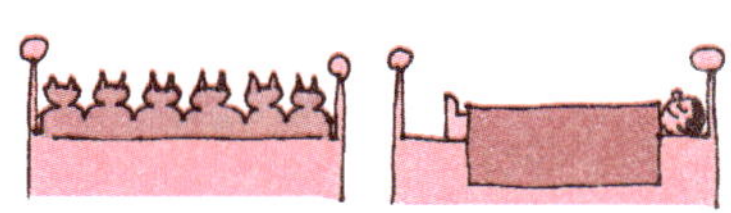

Max and the Tom Cats

Circle the words with the silent **"gh."**
Connect the circles to make a path.

Draw a line to the correct word, then write it.

Max, who is six,
sits up in a __________ .

tree

see

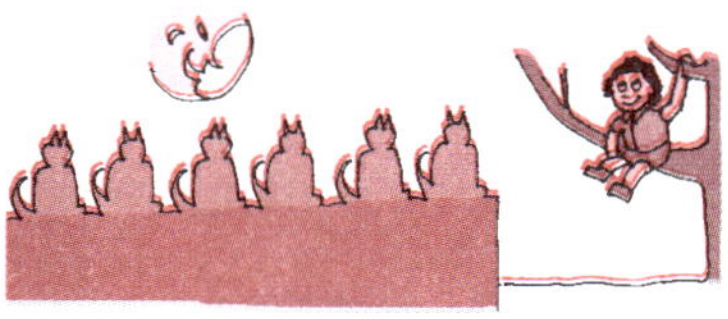

The man in the __________
saw six cats and Max.

soon

moon

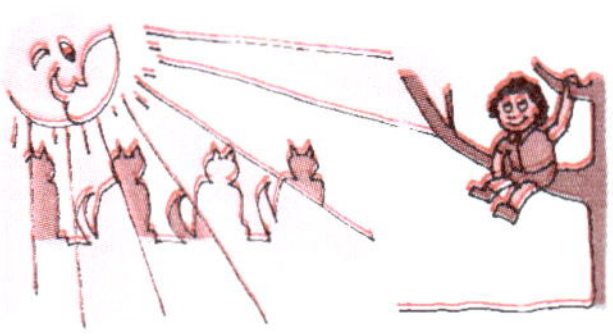

Soon the bright __________
of the moon sat over
them all.

light

sight

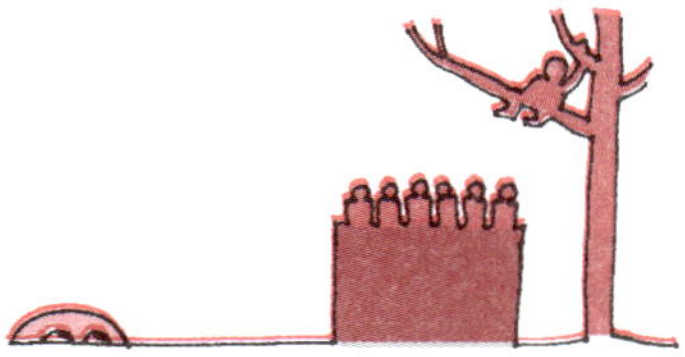

The song was over until
another __________ .

bright

night

Max and the Tom Cats

Put the words in the correct order to make the sentences.

to bed Max Go

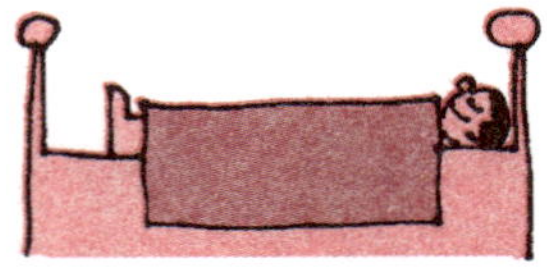

G _   _ _   _ _ _,

M _ _.

soon will sun The set

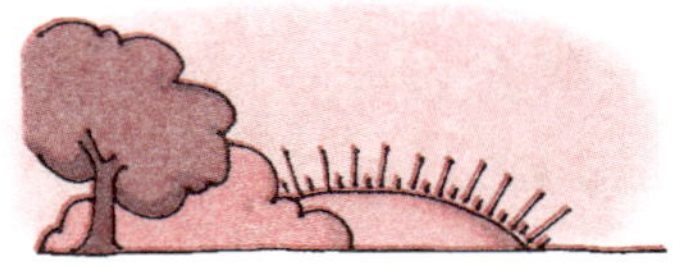

_ _ _   _ _ _   w _ _ _

_ _ _   _ _ _ _.

do see What you

W _ _ _   _ _

_ _ _   _ _ _?

Circle and write the correct consonant blend for each picture.

li ☐ t

ng mb gh gn

ni ☐

th ght ng tch

☐ ee

fr gr pr tr

☐ ight

br dr fr gr

Match the robots with their right shadows.

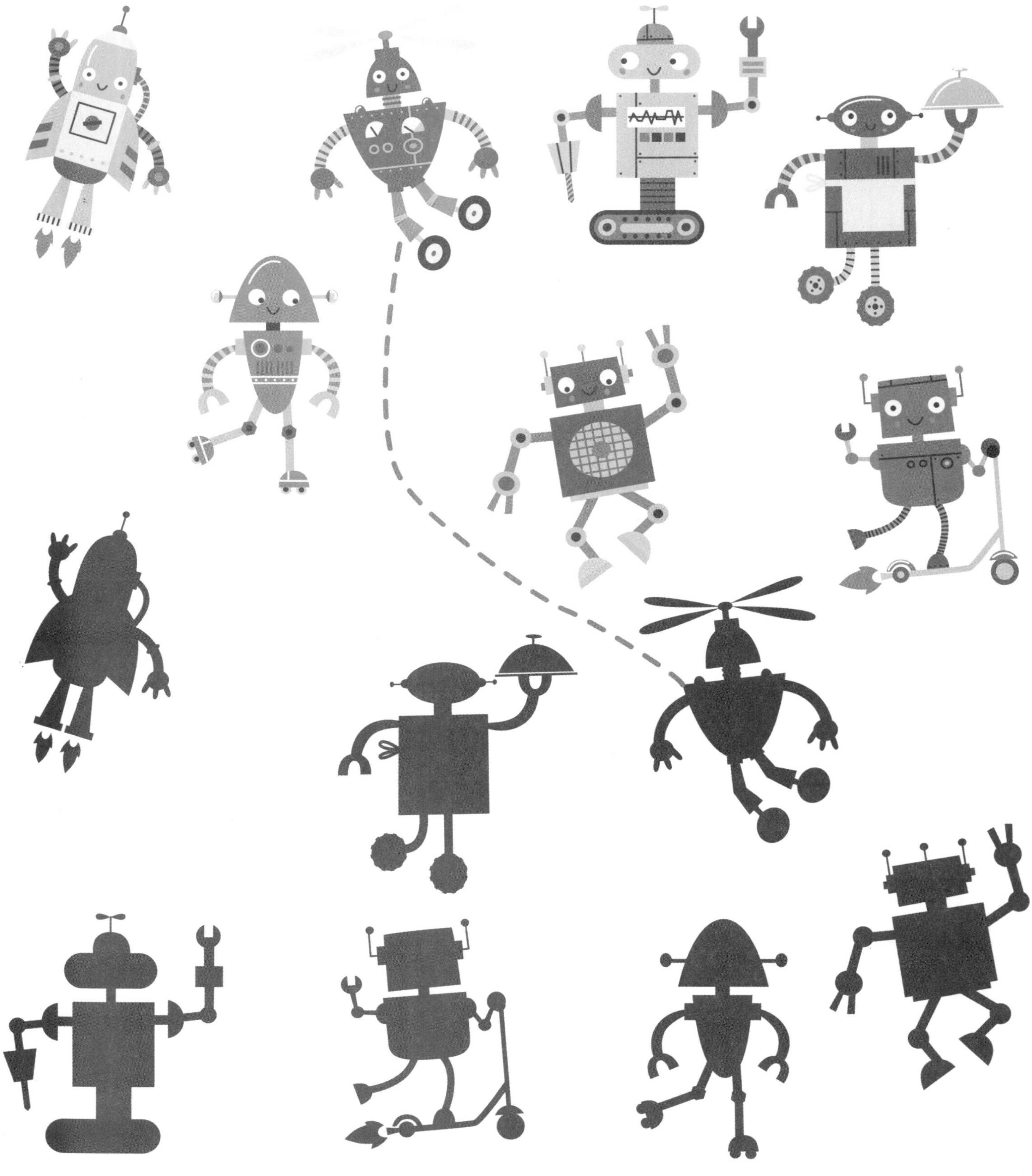

How many bugs of each type are there in this insect jumble? Write your answers in the circles below.

Only one of the bears can reach the honey. Who do you think is the lucky one?

Learn how to draw a ladybird.

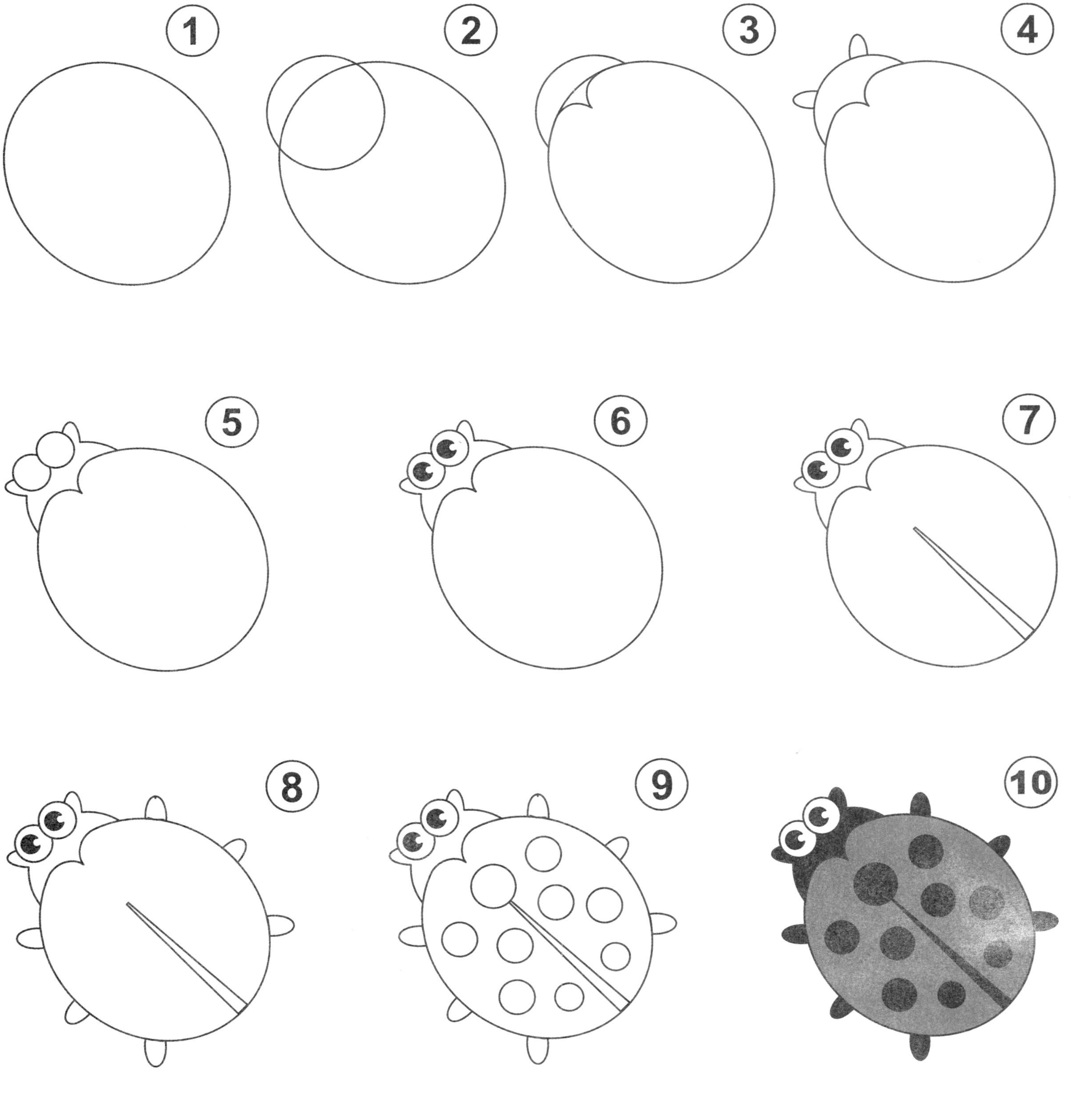

BOB BOOKS
SET 2
Advancing Beginners
SCHOLASTIC

STAGE 1: STARTING TO READ
BOB BOOKS
SET 1
SCHOLASTIC

BOB BOOKS
SET 3
Word Families
SCHOLASTIC

BOB BOOKS

STAGE 2: DEVELOPING READER
BOB BOOKS
SET 4
Complex Words
SCHOLASTIC

STAGE 1: STARTING TO READ
BOB BOOKS
More
Beginning Readers

STAGE 2: DEVELOPING READER
BOB BOOKS
SET 5
Long Vowels
SCHOLASTIC